CITY CYCLING
ANTWERP & GHENT

Rapha.

🔁 **Thames & Hudson**

Created by Andrew Edwards and Max Leonard of
Tandem London, a design, print and editorial studio

Thanks to Sebastiaan Van Doninck for illustrations;
Martijn van Egmond, *Soigneur* magazine and
totenmetontwerpen.nl; Fiona Mandos for a
Gentenaar's view; and Gregor Brown for his help
on Racing and Training

First published in the United Kingdom in 2013 by
Thames & Hudson Ltd, 181A High Holborn, London WC1V 7QX

City Cycling Antwerp & Ghent © 2013 Andrew Edwards and Max Leonard
Illustrations © 2013 Thames & Hudson Ltd, London and Rapha Racing Ltd

Designed by Andrew Edwards

Illustrations by Sebastiaan Van Doninck, sebastiaanvandoninck.be

British Library Cataloguing-in-Publication Data
A catalogue record for this book is available from the British Library

ISBN 978-0-500-29105-4

Printed and bound in China by Everbest Printing Co Ltd

To find out about all our publications, please visit
www.thamesandhudson.com. There you can subscribe
to our e-newsletter, browse or download our current catalogue,
and buy any titles that are in print.

CONTENTS

HOW TO USE THIS GUIDE

This volume of the *City Cycling* series covers Antwerp and Ghent, and is designed to give you the confidence to explore both cities by bike, at your own pace. Taking Antwerp first, on the front flaps is a locator map of the whole city to help you orient yourself. We've divided the city up into four different neighbourhoods: Centrum (p. 10); Schipperskwartier and 't Eilandje (p. 18); Diamantkwartier and De Zurenborg (p. 24); and Zuid (p. 30). Then, after another map showing both cities, there's an extended neighbourhood guide to Ghent (p. 38). All of the areas are easily accessible by bike, and are full of cafés, bars, galleries, museums, shops and parks. Each neighbourhood is mapped in detail, and our recommendations for places of interest and where to fuel up on coffee and cake, as well as where to find a Wi-Fi connection, are marked. Take a pootle round on your bike and see what suits you.

The neighbourhood maps also show bike routes, bike shops and landmarks – everything you need to navigate safely and pinpoint specific locations across a large section of the centre of town. If you fancy a set itinerary, turn to A Day On The Bike, also on the front flaps. It takes you on a relaxed 25km (16-mile) route through some of the parts of Antwerp we haven't featured in the neighbourhood sections, and visits some of the more touristy sights. Pick and choose the bits you fancy, go from back to front, and use the route as it suits you.

A section on Racing and Training (p. 48) fills you in on some of Antwerp and Ghent's long cycling heritage and provides ideas for longer rides if you want to explore the beautiful countryside around the cities, while Essential Bike Info (p. 54) discusses road etiquette and the ins and outs of navigating your way along Belgium's cycle routes. Finally, Links and Addresses (p. 58) will give you the practical details you need to know.

ANTWERP & GHENT: THE CYCLING CITIES

Antwerp and Ghent are, behind Brussels, the second and third biggest cities in Belgium, but in cyclists' hearts the Belgian capital is a distant third. The Dutch-speaking province of Flanders, and Ghent in particular, is the heartland of continental road cycling. Many professional cyclists live in and around Ghent – host of the first significant one-day race in the annual cycling calendar – and you'll likely spot some serious riders whenever you're there; see the Racing and Training section (p. 48) for more.

It's not just pro racing, however, that attracts cyclists to Flanders. The province, perhaps even more so than the country's Wallonian south, shares the Dutch enthusiasm for everyday cycling, and Antwerp and Ghent are two cities – one small, and the other very small – that are built on a bicycle's scale. Ghent used to be congested and dirty, but, after 15 years of enlightened policy-making that put the bicycle first, it now has more than 300km (186 miles) of bike lanes tracking its roads, canals and rivers. Upon arriving at Gent-Sint-Pieters station, a sea of bikes will greet you. Cycle up into town, and you'll be pedalling, with scores of other cyclists, along a segregated bike path before joining the trams on the cobbled streets of the largest car-free city centre in Europe.

Antwerp, too, has a fair number of students, but it is larger and, for its size, very diverse, with Jewish, African and Middle Eastern populations contributing to the mix. The bicycle may stand out less, but facilities for cyclists are very good; in 2012, Antwerp's mayor, realizing he had promised 100km (62 miles) of new bike lanes in his second term, embarked upon a major construction programme before an imminent election. Despite losing, his efforts contributed to the already high quality of provision for cyclists: all traffic-heavy roads have segregated bike lanes. In both cities, cycling is firmly embedded in everyday life. Around 16 per cent of commuting journeys in Antwerp are by bike; in Ghent, it is 19 per cent. Both are extremely friendly places and, even where cyclists share the road with motorists, you can expect to be waved through roundabouts and treated with respect. There's not the huge crush of daredevil cyclists you'll find in Amsterdam or Copenhagen, but that's all the better if you just want to cruise around and see the sights. And both places try to make cycling fun. Ride along <u>Coupure Links</u> in Ghent, for example, and you'll pass a digital display unit counting the number of cyclists that have passed by that day, week and year – you'll become another digit in the Belgian cycling revolution.

Each city, dense with roads, shops, culture and sights, offers more than enough to keep you riding round for a weekend or longer. In the Middle Ages, Ghent was the second largest city in Europe after Paris, powered by a galloping textile industry that thrived on the flat, fertile lands around it. Antwerp later rose to prominence after Bruges' harbour silted up, and the important shipping trade moved east. Although Antwerp was heavily shelled in the Second World War, both cities retain their historic centres and beautiful buildings. Ghent is the more perfect, but it seems naturally vibrant and to attract a slightly 'alternative' crowd: it has more vegetarian restaurants per head than anywhere in Europe, and promotes to its residents a 'meat-free' day each week. Perhaps, also, the students – around one-fifth of the population – rescue it from being twee.

While Ghent's connections to textiles are long in the past, it is to the rag trade, or rather haute couture, that Antwerp owes its renaissance as a European hub of cool. In the 1980s a golden generation of designers including Dries Van Noten, Ann Demeulemeester and Walter Van Beirendonck made this northern port city their home. The so-called 'Antwerp Six' added a dynamic edge to a place already known for its gemstones, architecture and historic monuments; today, Antwerp is a centre of design, avant-garde art, fashion and food, with fantastic vintage shopping. It may sound pretentious – and apparently Belgians from elsewhere view *Antwerpenaars* as stuck up – but in reality it's very down to earth: the influence of the huge working docks keeps the city's feet firmly on the ground.

Visit Antwerp and Ghent singly, or as a pair, and you won't be disappointed. And take some time to explore around them: there are links to training loops in the Racing and Training section, or the Tourist Office in either city will supply very good maps of cycle routes in the surrounding countryside for only a small cost.

NEIGHBOURHOODS

CENTRUM

BARS, RESTAURANTS AND BEAUTIFUL
HISTORIC BUILDINGS

At the heart of Antwerp, between its smart suburbs, river and working docks, lies a beautiful city centre built on the riches brought about by centuries of trading. The area is bounded by Frankrijklei to the east; by Klapdorp, in the north, it's shading into the Schipperskwartier (p. 18); and by Muntstraat in the south you're almost in the Zuid (p. 30). The Scheldt river lies to the west, and the cycle path that runs along the quayside is a great expressway to get quickly from one side of town to another. You'll see architectural highlights, too, such as local architect Bob van Reeth's café, **Zuiderterras** ①.

Cycle through the <u>Grote Markt</u> early in the morning as the church bells chime the hour (at the weekends before all the tourists arrive), and it's as if the centuries haven't passed at all. On one side is the impressive **Stadhuis** ②; facing it, a row of cafés and bars

occupy ornate guild houses with their tall, narrow Low Country frontages. **Café Noord** ③ is a classic Belgian bistro, which, despite its tourist-drawing location, serves brilliant food. Just round the corner is another tourist hotspot – **'t Elfde Gebod** ④, possibly the holiest bar in the world. Settle in, admire the hundreds of statues of madonnas and saints, and order a Duvel ('devil') beer.

Not far away is another local favourite, **Café Beveren** ⑤, populated by a mix of sailors, students and tourists, with a magnificent old organ (of the self-playing variety), which must be seen to be believed. North of Grote Markt (which, by the way, is where you'll find **Frituur No. 1** ⑥, for traditional Belgian fries), it becomes especially interesting around Palingbrug, Veemarkt and Zirkstraat, where you'll find sympathetically designed new apartment blocks, and a warren of bike-friendly paths between the sixteenth-century windows. There's also the university, on <u>Blindestraat</u>, which resembles an Oxford college in its quiet studiousness. Another tranquil spot is **Sint-Jacobskerk** ⑦, best known as the location of Rubens's tomb. Above it hangs *Our Lady, surrounded by saints*, which features Rubens himself as St George. Less solemn are the bars and pubs of the area; **'t Waagstuk** ⑧, with its formidable selection of Belgian beer, is one of our recommendations. In between, **Bike Project** ⑨ and **Fixerati** ⑩ will help you out with any bike parts you might need.

Other lovely, quiet squares in the centre include the <u>Vrijdagmarkt</u>, where you'll find the **Plantin-Moretus Museum** ⑪, devoted to typography and print, in the former workshop of two of Belgium's most famous Renaissance printers, Christophe Plantin and Jan Moretus. Head to <u>Hendrik Conscienceplein</u> and you might get lucky and find **Nottebohm** ⑫ open – a fantastic private library, now owned by the city, which is only rarely accessible by the public. If you can't get in there, try **'t Brantyser** ⑬, a traditional Belgian bistro, also on the square, or for a quicker, if not lighter, bite, **Bakkerij Goossens** ⑭, a patisserie where the number of people waiting testify to the quality.

Finally, two contrasting museums to finish the central tour, both of which reflect modern Antwerp's influences: **Museum Mayer van den Bergh** ⑮, full of paintings, sculptures and tapestries from antiquity to the eighteenth century, collected by a businessman with an eye for a bargain; and **ModeMuseum** ⑯, a fashion museum with pieces from the sixteenth century to the Antwerp Six and beyond. Next door is **ModeNatie** ⑰, housing the Flanders Fashion Institute, and the fashion, art and design bookshop, Copyright.

REFUELLING

FOOD	DRINK
Désiré de Lille ⑱ for the finest Belgian waffles	**Kulminator** ⑳ has been called the best place for beer in Belgium
Lombardia ⑲ is a colourful, bustling organic café	**Grand Café Horta** ㉑ next to Theaterplein for a grand experience

WI-FI
McQueen ㉒ serves serious coffee and waffles while you surf

22

22

22

THONET LA...

FREDERIK VAN EEDENPLEIN

FREDERIK VAN EEDENPLEIN

SINT-ANNATUNNEL

...NLAAN

STEEN...

WANDELTERRAS ZUID

HA...

5

1

ZAND

S...

4

...SVL...

RIJKENHOEK

OEVER

MUNT...

...HOU...

3

SINT-JANSVLIET

PLANTINLAAN

2

KLOOSTERSTRAAT

ST-MICHIELS STRAAT

3 mi

1/2 km

1/2 m

ARSENAALSTRAAT

34

KORTE VLIERSTR...

LA...

34

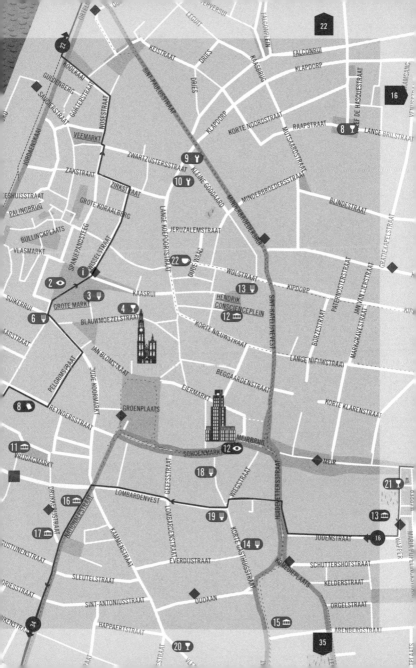

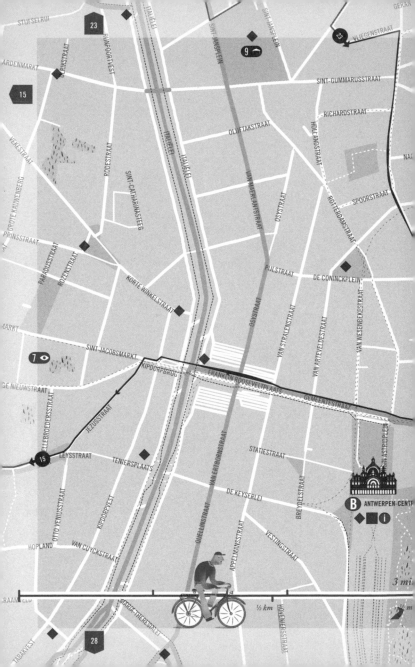

SCHIPPERSKWARTIER & 'T EILANDJE

DOCKS, REGENERATION, RELAXATION

Head north out of the sixteenth-century centre, and Antwerp's status as Europe's second-largest port becomes more apparent. Its huge, busy working dock is almost in the centre of town, stretching all the way to Holland, and gives the surrounding areas a vibrant, slightly rough-and-ready feel. Yes, there's a red-light district here (centred around <u>Verversrui</u>, where you'll find **Café d'Anvers** ①, one of Europe's leading dance-music venues), but there are also vintage shops, museums and huge regeneration projects that are turning 't Eilandje ('the little island') into a buzzing part of the city.

Closer to the heart of Antwerp, the historic Schipperskwartier (skippers' quarter) is full of picturesque warehouse buildings, some now converted into apartments and studios, and home to the city's mobile design and fashion crowd. Take a ride through the streets around <u>Falconrui</u> at dusk, and peek through the lighted windows around you. Some houses and pubs have lifebelts mounted on the walls; others, as you get closer to the old town, intricately carved statues of the Virgin and Child – two ways of assuring salvation. Head to the pretty **Sint-Paulusplaats** ② for a drink or, for vintage furniture and homeware, to **Second Life** ③. The nearby **Dock's Café** ④ is a classic, if expensive, baroque bistro, frequented by dockers and businessmen alike.

Further north, you're confronted by the harbour and the landmark **Museum Aan de Stroom** ⑤, known as MAS, designed by Dutch architects Neutelings Riedijk and celebrating Antwerp's long history as a port. Climb to the roof for a free view of the whole city and Luc Tuymans's mosaic, *Dead Skull*, below. The in-house café Storm is pleasant, but you can try any in its shadow across the road (for breakfast, we recommend **Waanzee** ⑥). **Espressobar Broer Bretel** ⑦ is just to the north, and not far away are 't Fritkotje ⑧, a traditional Belgian frites takeaway, and **Eetcafé Cabo Verde** ⑨, for something more exotic. For a drink in the evening sun, try **Bocadero** ⑩ – hidden behind warehouses and cranes, it's a cool hangout with great views over the Scheldt.

Also celebrating the history of the area is the new **Red Star Line Museum** ⑪, housed in the company's former warehouses, which tells the story of the famous passenger ships that transported hundreds of thousands of migrants from Europe to New York and Philadelphia. Across the water is another boat, **Badboot** ⑫, though this one is now a floating swimming pool and café. It's one of the signs of major regeneration in the area, as is the **Sint-Felix warehouse** ⑬, an important harbour building that is now a public archive, renovated by architects Robbrecht & Daem to include an internal public street.

Though things are changing, it's worth exploring the whole area by bike for an authentic taste of life on the waterfront – proper dockers' cafés, ships coming in and out of the harbour, active warehouses for shifting goods. Many of the streets, such as <u>Indiestraat</u>, have very rough cobbles, so your ride will be juddery – be careful not to catch thin tyres in the gaps. Alternatively, head up <u>Noorderlaan</u> and take a left on <u>Groendaallaan,</u> looping back via <u>Stratsburgbrug</u> and <u>Mexicostraat</u> for a good view of 't Eilandje and the old town behind it. Finally, for some relaxation, head to **Park Spoor Noord** ⑭, a former goods yard that is now a lively public space with a great playground for children and its own open-air bar, **Cargo** ⑮.

REFUELLING

FOOD	DRINK
Caravan Eetcafé ⑯, tucked away in a three-cornered square	**NormoCoffee** ⑱ offers some of the city's best coffee
Het Pomphuis ⑰ is a spectacular Art Nouveau setting for a bite to eat	

WI-FI
Yellow Submarine ⑲ is a modern B&B with a café and free surfing

3 mins

½ km

½ mile

MERANTISTRAAT

STRAATSBURGDOK-ZUIDKAAI

TJALKSTRAAT

KAMBALASTRAAT

HOUTDOK-NOORDKAAI

JAVIESTRAAT

NOORDKASTEEL-OOST

VIILESTRAAT

NOORDERLAAN

STEENBORGERWEERT

MERKSEMSESTRAAT

MADRASSTRAAT

IJZERLAAN

IJZERLAAN

IJZERLAAN

NOORDSCHIPPERSKAAI

BOMBAYSTRAAT

INDIËSTRAAT

SAMGA STEENHOUWERSVEST

DWARSDIJK NOORDKASTEEL

SAMGASTRAAT

DRIESMELLENSTRAAT

16

DAMPLEIN

GENUASTRAAT

KEMPISCHDOK-WESTKAAI

KADIXSTRAAT

STRAAT

DAMPLEIN

IJZERLAAN-OOST

BRUGENSTRAAT

RIGASTRAAT

AUGUST MICHIELSSTRAAT

KEMPENSTRAAT

HARDEVOORT

15

LOS DEN WIND

DAMPLEIN

LONDENSTRAAT

NOORDERLAAN

14

PARK SPOOR NOORD

PARK SPOOR NOORD

8

9

NOORDERLAAN

ELLERMANSTRAAT

SINT-LAZARUSSTRAAT

KEMPENDOKSTRAAT

ENTREPOTDOKKAAI

DUBOISSTRAAT

ZUIDERSTRAAT

KORTE DIJKSTRAAT

TREPTSTRAAT

ORANJESTRAAT

BILKORSTRAAT

KLAMPESTEENWEG

DE WAGHEMAKERSTRAAT

VAN AERDSTRAAT

MARNIXSTRAAT

TULPSTRAAT

SINT-ANNASTRAAT

EVERAERTSSTRAAT

TUNNELPLAATS

TUNNELPLAATS

SCHIJNPOORTWEG

KEILINCKSTRAAT

LANGE DIJKSTRAAT

ZIRKSTRAAT

DANREMSTRAAT

GEERAARD SEGERSSTRAAT

GERANIUMSTRAAT

TULPSTRAAT

MORGENSTRAAT

LANGE LOBROEKSTRAAT

9

VLIEGENSTRAAT

KLIPSTRAAT

MAALDERIJSTRAAT

MAALDERIJSTRAAT

PIONIERSSTRAAT

WILGENSTRAAT

STIJFSELRUI

PAARDENMARKT

SINT-GUMMARUSSTRAAT

RICHARDSTRAAT

LANGE VAN STERBEECKSTRAAT

LANGE SCHOLIERSSTRAAT

BRILSTRAAT

OLIFANTSTRAAT

MOLLANDSTRAAT

NACHTEGAALSTRAAT

16

KORTE ZALELSTRAAT

16

SPOORSTRAAT

DIAMANTKWARTIER & DE ZURENBORG

BELLE EPOQUE GEMS

Travel the streets of De Zurenborg, and you'll marvel that it was once almost levelled and covered with modern houses and offices. The area – bounded by <u>Plantin en Moretuslei</u> to the north and the amazing, castellated railway lines to the west, along with the Antwerp ring road – was the only part of the city to be developed as a piece. During the final decades of the nineteenth century and before the start of the First World War in 1914, some very noted architects produced landmark homes for the city's bourgeoisie in a riot of styles, ideas and colours. But as car use grew and the middle classes moved to the suburbs, the large houses became unloved and threatened with

demolition. Protests by local residents and artists gained a stay of execution, and today the majority are restored and in fine form.

Less on display are the riches of the **Diamantkwartier** ①, just south of the beautiful **Antwerpen-Centraal** ②, itself an essential sight. Built in marble and gold, and with arrivals and departures stacked up on different levels, the railway station is weirdly dreamlike and reminiscent of an Escher sketch. Antwerp has been a centre of the diamond trade since Lodewyk van Berken invented a new type of diamond-cutter in the fifteenth century, producing the multifaceted gems we know today. In the modern age, the trade is dominated by the Indian and Hasidic Jewish communities (there is a large population of the latter in Antwerp, which has been traditionally concentrated in this area). <u>Pelikaanstraat</u> is the Diamantkwartier's public face, but the real action takes place behind closed doors in <u>Hovenierstraat,</u> surrounded by hi-tech security. Take a look at the rock-polishing equipment in the shops around the **International Gemological Institute** ③; if you wait long enough, you may see people hurrying past, briefcases handcuffed to their wrists, and other signs of the fortunes bought and sold in the four trading exchanges.

For green space, head to the peaceful **Stadspark** ④. Nearby are some fascinating antiques and vintage shops ⑤, as well as **Hoffy's** ⑥, known as one of the best kosher kitchens in Europe. For more upmarket eating, head under the railway to a cute street corner where the Dôme empire presides. Created by a French chef and a former stylist for Dries Van Noten, eateries include **Dôme** ⑦ and acclaimed fish restaurant **Dôme sur Mer** ⑧, as well as a bakery, **Domestic** ⑨. Head west and you'll soon find <u>Dageraadplaats</u>, a large square surrounded by cafés and restaurants – we recommend **Zeezicht** ⑩ for

a terrace where, in the summer, you can watch free music events. On a smaller scale is <u>Draakplaats</u>, a charming square dominated by a railway line and tram shed, where you'll find **Café Vertigo** ⑪, a bar with good music and a vast selection of whiskeys (as well as Wi-Fi; see below), and **Moskou** ⑫, which also does a fine brunch.

To the south, <u>Cogels-Osylei</u> is a glorious jumble of architectural styles: Jugendstil, neo-Baroque, Gothic revival, Art Nouveau, almost any fin-de-siècle movement you can think of. It's as if the architects, principally Joseph Bascourt, Jules Hofman and Frans Smet-Verhas, were competing to outdo each other. Don't forget to check out the treasures in surrounding streets, including the **Four Seasons houses** ⑬ (four buildings facing each other on a crossroads), or the **Battle of Waterloo mosaic** ⑭, sprawled across a building façade, with its portraits of Napoleon and Nelson. <u>Velodroomstraat</u>, meanwhile, hints at the former location of Antwerp's world-famous 'Garden City' velodrome, which is no more.

REFUELLING

FOOD	DRINK
Réfectoire ⑮ does exquisite food in a low-key, atmospheric setting	**Caffènation** ⑯: three floors of coffee at Antwerp's original coffee hipster joint

WI-FI
The Wi-Fi signal at **Café Vertigo** ⑪ extends to its sunny terrace

Cycle south from the centre, and the hustle and bustle begins to dissipate as you enter the narrow streets of the Sint-Andries neighbourhood. When the streets become wider again, you'll know you're in the Zuid. Here, the pace of life is relaxed and opulent: it's an area to come to for a beer in the sunshine on <u>Marnixplaats</u> or a glass of wine at **Vinicity** ①, an evening of live jazz at **Café Hopper** ② or an afternoon of shopping at the flagship stores of local fashion heroes **Dries Van Noten** ③ and **Ann Demeulemeester** ④.

Zuid, as explored here, is bounded to the east by Amerikalei and Britselei, and gets going towards the southern ends of <u>Nationalestraat</u>

and <u>Kloosterstraat</u> – Antwerp's twin centres of, respectively, fashion and vintage design. On Kloosterstraat, you may want to stop at **Your** ⑤, an emporium with a bit of everything, including bicycles, fashion, books, even a hairdressing salon. Its sister store **Noë** ⑥ specializes in women's accessories and shoes. Cycle down Nationalestraat, taking a left when it forks at the bottom, and you'll hit prime drinking and dining territory – **Fiskebar** ⑦ is one of Antwerp's favourite, and most affordable, fish restaurants.

The right fork will take you bumping down the cobbled <u>Volkstraat</u>, with its gloriously tiled **Steinerschool** ⑧, to **Coffee &**

Vinyl ⑨, a bright, comfortable café with a backroom treasure trove of records. It's one more fusion in an area that seems full of concept stores and interestingly jumbled-up shopping experiences. RA (see A Day On The Bike) is one; Hospital ⑩ is another. Its warehouse contains 1,200m² (12,917 sq ft) of men's and women's fashion from local and international designers, and is flanked by a restaurant, wine bar and luxury B&B. Across the road, Clinic ⑪ gives streetwear the same treatment. Almost every parade of shops in the Zuid contains chic boutiques that are ripe for browsing, such as FCS (Furniture and Clothing Selection) ⑫, whose wares are drawn from the best vintage sources. Further north, the designs of Walter Van Beirendonck are showcased at Walter ⑬, housed in a former garage.

In the southwest of the neighbourhood lies Gedempte Zuiderdokken ⑭, an open space where the annual *Bollekesfeest* of Flemish food and culture is held every August (*een bolleke* is the glass used to hold the local beer, De Koninck, so it's easy to guess what happens when the festival comes around). During the rest of the year the area's many museums are the main attraction, including MuHKA

⑮, Antwerp's celebrated modern art museum; the **FotoMuseum** ⑯ with its great bookshop; and **KMSKA** (Royal Museum of Fine Arts) ⑰, which presides over the nearby <u>Leopold de Waelplaats</u>. Also close by is **Revista** ⑱, a good coffee place if you need to catch your breath, and **Chatleroi** ⑲, a more traditional café that attracts the in-crowd in the evenings. Or try **L'Entrepôt du Congo** ⑳ for relaxed, retro café style in a beautiful building, or **Haute Frituur** ㉑, a *frietkoten* (chip shop) that serves excellent Belgian frites in style. **Sips** ㉒ is the place to end your day in the Zuid, as it serves some of Antwerp's best cocktails; just be sure to see the Richard Rogers-designed **Antwerps Justitiepaleis** ㉓, known locally as the *Vlinderpaleis* (butterfly palace) because of its rippling, wing-like roof, before the sun goes down.

REFUELLING

FOOD	DRINK
Walrus ㉔ is a local haunt with international food **De Biologisch-Dynamische Bakkerij** ㉕ for lunch, breakfast and organic baked goods	**Starfish & Coffee** ㉖ is a cosy café with soup, cakes and homemade ginger tea

WI-FI
King Kong ㉗ is a slick, stylish bar with free wireless

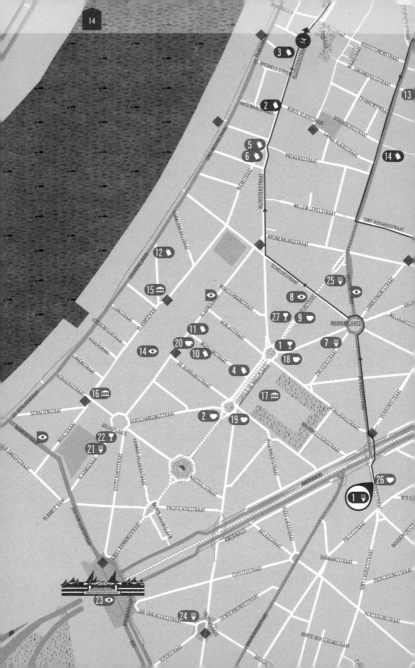

3 mins

½ km   ½ mile

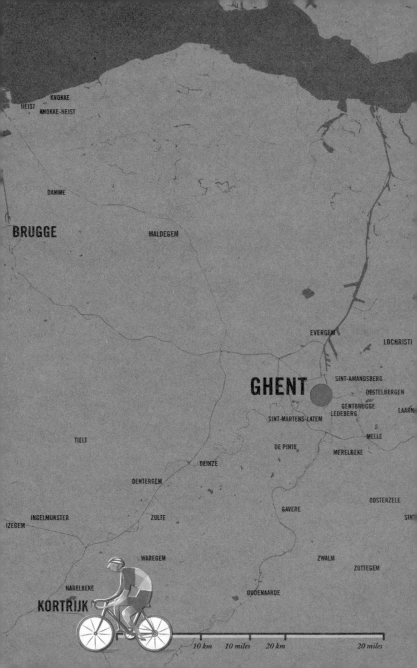

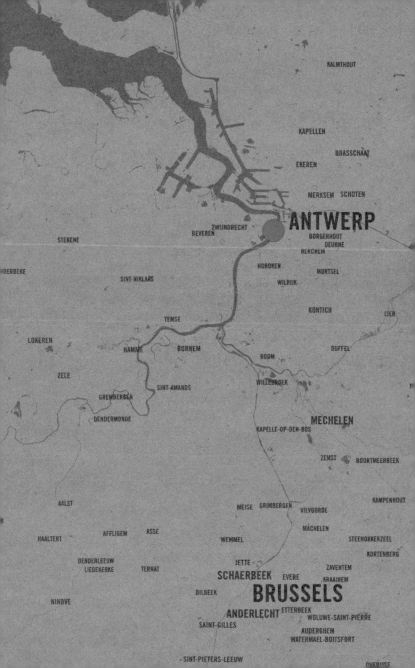

GHENT

A BIKE-SIZED CHUNK OF EXCEPTIONAL
HISTORY, CULTURE, FOOD AND FUN

Now that the cars have been banished from the city centre, cycling round Ghent's medieval buildings, canal and rivers is a glorious experience. We'll start in the middle of the historic splendour at **Oud Huis Himschoot** ① for a local cinnamon pastry known as a *mastel*. Pair it with a coffee from **Mokabon** ②, and take your loot away for an al-fresco breakfast on the **Graslei** ③ – the classic canalside hangout for locals, tourists and students alike – while you plan your day. (If it's raining, **Brooderie** ④, a café and tearoom close by, is a good refuge.) After breakfast, head to **Sint-Baafskathedraal** ⑤ before the crowds arrive to gawp at Hubert and Jan van Eyck's altarpiece,

painted in the fifteenth century. Nearby, <u>Hoogpoort</u> is home to independent shops such as **Suite** ⑥ for women's fashion, and **Toykyo** ⑦, the boutique of Ghent's eponymous creative agency.

For antiques and vintage finds, there are several hotspots. The **Antiek Depot** ⑧ is a treasure trove for browsing, with two floors of paintings, furniture and other objets d'art ranging from the truly valuable to the merely old. On <u>Bij Sint-Jacobs</u>, a flea market is held in the shadow of **Sint-Jacobskerk** ⑨ on Saturdays and Sundays. Occasionally some real finds can be uncovered among the odds and ends, so have a rummage, then grab a coffee at the French-styled

Dépôt Central ⑩ and contemplate your bargaining strategy. Just along <u>Steendam</u> is **Het Archief** ⑪, with its range of vintage design and antiques; for more modern interiors, head to **Surplus** ⑫. This western part of town is home to Ghent's design and illustration school, so it's an arty quarter that's worth a pedal around.

WANDERING THROUGH THE NORTH

Across the Leie to the north and west of the old town centre, the first thing you'll encounter is **Gravensteen Castle** ⑬, where the roads form a pinch-point for cars and trams (watch out for trams, even in the car-free areas and in the main squares). <u>Kraanlei</u> and <u>Oudberg</u> are some of the most picturesque – and bumpy – cobbled streets in the old town, with beautiful views across the river. They're still within prime tourist territory, so you'll find quirky shops like **The Fallen Angels** ⑭, full of old advertising and movie posters, and **Ydee** ⑮, which features a collection of furniture from young designers. If you need a break, **Barista** ⑯ does good coffee and cake, and **Het Velootje Gent** ⑰ is a must-see for bike fans. Push open the nondescript front door and you'll find a bike workshop-cum-bar, where owner Lieven De Vos has been serving beers, surrounded by bits of his vintage bike collection, for twenty-five years. Opening hours are irregular, so try later on in the evenings. If you prefer something healthier, head to **Aqua Azul** ⑱, a sauna and spa in a stunning Art Nouveau building.

The pretty roads become smaller and quieter the further you get into the Patershol neighbourhood, but to really get away from it all, **Holy Corner** ⑲ is a must. <u>Begijnhofdries</u> was one of Ghent's three *begijnhofs* – church-run communities for devout single women – and, although it's social housing now, the walled gardens and enclosed square are still beautiful, as is the rustic <u>Provenierstraat</u>, just south. Further north, the crumbling architecture and quaint, cobbled canal-side streets continue. Be sure to head to <u>Prinsenhofplein</u>, along <u>Zilverhof</u> and over the **Charles Bridge** ⑳, nicknamed the 'bridge of imperial pleasures'. Guarded by knights on horseback atop columns, it was used, or so the story goes, by the mistresses of Emperor Charles V in the sixteenth century to access his chambers at night. Head even further north, and the area becomes more industrial. <u>Dok Noord</u> is still very pretty, and offers good views past the boats and seagulls to the old working-class neighbourhood of Muide.

MUSEUMS AND GREEN SPACES

Walking through certain areas of central Ghent can feel like being in a living museum, so exceptional are the surroundings. And hidden away among the historic buildings are several museums of note. **Design Museum Gent** ㉑ contains seventeenth and eighteenth-century furnishings and interiors, as well as examples of Art Deco, Art Nouveau and contemporary design. **Sint-Pietersabdij** ㉒, a former Benedictine abbey, has beautiful gardens and hosts photography and art exhibitions; it's also close to **Quetzal** ㉓, a Belgian chocolate café. **SMAK** ㉔ is the city's modern art museum, with a reputation for bold programming. It's next to **Citadelpark** ㉕, the largest and prettiest park in town (though not to be visited at night).

For more open spaces, head along <u>Watersportlaan</u>, an area popular with *Gentenaars* for jogging and other outdoor pursuits. The **Cycling Centre Eddy Merckx** ㉖ is just off-map; if you're on a city bike, a better idea is to lock it up and have a swim at **Blaarmeersen** ㉗, where all of Ghent seems to congregate on sunny days. North of Waterspoortlaan (mainly off-map) is **Bourgoyen-Ossemeersen** ㉘, a huge nature reserve right next to the city. Alternatively, if you're on

the opposite side of town, head to **Het Hinkelspel** ㉙, a bread and cheese-making co-operative, and then down the canal for a picnic. Visserij is a picturesque route along the row of houseboats, or follow the tangling waterways until you find a quiet, sunny spot.

On this eastern side, you'll find **DOK** ㉚, an alternative arts and performance space, surrounded by cranes and derelict industrial buildings. In the summer, its sandy beach and canteen rival any of the hippest underground spots in Amsterdam or Berlin. It's a relaxed hangout, and the perfect place to watch the world go by.

EVENING PLANS

Start the evening off with a drink at **Gruut Stadsbrouwerij** ㉛, a recently established brewery located on a pretty waterside corner. Or to catch up on the latest cycling gossip, head to **Café De Karper** ㉜, run by a local cycling family (see also p. 53, in the Racing and Training section). **Bord'eau** ㉝, an upmarket restaurant, has stunning views over the water, while **Komkommertijd** ㉞, a healthy vegetarian buffet with surprising combinations of flavours and ingredients, is a more low-key option. **Mosquito Coast** ㉟ is popular with locals for both cocktails and food, and **Den Turk** ㊱, just round the corner, is a traditional 'brown' bar, well known for being the oldest jazz and blues bar in town. For after-hours fun, there's **Charlatan** ㊲ on Vlasmarkt, and *Gentenaars* also head to Oude Beestenmarkt – try **Café Video** ㊳.

REFUELLING

FOOD	DRINK
Lekker GEC ㊴, a vegetarian buffet near the station	**Marimain** ㊸ has a terrace that is a favourite local suntrap – good for a beer
Frituur Jozef ㊵ for Belgian fries the old-fashioned way	**Huize Colette** ㊹ for chocolate specialities with books on the shelves
Le Jardin Bohémien ㊶: coffee, brunch – and vintage furniture	**Café De Loge** ㊺ is a friendly place in the west
Damme Patisserie ㊷ for baked goods	**OR Espressobar** ㊻ for a good coffee

WI-FI
Pain Perdu ㊼, a relaxed local café where you can while the hours away
Vooruit ㊽ is a performance venue and gallery with a Wi-Fi-enabled café

PULSTRAAT

KRUUL HOOFDPULBELKESTRAAT

KONINGINNELAAN

HEILIG BLOEDSTRAAT

EEKERGEMSTRAAT

SEBASTIAANSVELD

HAAS VAN GAVERESTRAAT

RUITHAVENSTRAAT

BERNARD SPRIELAAN

MASTELLANELAAN

CHARLES ANDRIESLAAN

28

26

27

VLIERDENSE BRIEDELAAN

KUITEMARTINSTRAAT

ROOISTRAAT

BUIL DREVEL

ZUIDERLIELAN

BLOSSTRAAT

NEERMEERSKAAI

ZUIDERDOORGANG

KAAI

SPORTSTRAAT

PATHIERSTRAAT

MANDRALSTRAAT

DISTELSTRAAT

AUGEMSTRAAT

PROSPER CLAEYSTRAAT

RAKETSTRAAT

MEIRSTRAAT

PAUL FREDERICQSTRAAT

IPERLAAN

NOORDOORGANG

GROTE BRITANNIEKHOF

ABDIJSTRAAT

MARTELAARSLAAN

LOUIS PASTEURLAAN

NEERMEERSKAAI

HANS VAN MARKESTRAAT

PROSPER CLAEYSTRAAT

DESIRE VAN MONCKHOVENSTRAAT

EVANS DE POTTERSTRAAT

KONINGIN ELISABETHLAAN

KONINGIN ASTRIDLAAN

B GENT-SINT-PIETERS

39

HENDRIK VAN BRESSCKOVENSTRAAT

LAMORAAL VAN EGMONTSTRAAT

EDELM VAN NASSAUSTRAAT

BALIESTRAAT

SINT-PAULUSSTRAAT

IEPER VAN MARNIXSTRAAT

ZONDERDOORGANG

LAURENT DELVAUXSTRAAT

32

25

24

3 mins

½ mile

THERESIANENSTRAAT

SCHOUWVEGERSSTRAAT

JAN VAN STOPENBERGE

WILDEROOSSTRAAT

12

JONKVROUW MATTESTRAAT

ZWARTEZUSTERSSTRAAT

DOBIJNENSTEEG HOORN

WELLINGSTRAAT

BRANDSTRAAT

PUSSEMEERSTRAAT

CASINOPLEIN

CALGEMBERG

PAPEGAAISTRAAT

TWAALFKAMEREN

MAAGDESTRAAT

45

ANNONCIADENSTR

ZANDPOORTSTRAAT

KOPERSTRAAT

KROMMENELLEBOOG

PEKELHARING

SINT-AGNETESTRAAT

WIJNGAARDSTRAAT

TIEBAERTSTEEG

SINT-BAERTSTEEG

APOTHEEKSTRAAT

IJZET KLUTDENSTRAAT

BILCKVELD

VELDSTRAAT

RACING AND TRAINING

THE CLASSICS AND TRAINING RIDES

To say that cycle racing is like a religion in Belgium would be a bit of an understatement, with the Flemish even more fanatical than their Wallonian neighbours. From the back-to-back semi-Classics on the opening weekend of the European season to the Brabantse Pijl in mid-April, Flanders is gripped each spring with cycle-racing fever. Barely has the mud settled on the cyclocross season, and the boards stopped vibrating at the velodromes after the winter Six Day races, before road-racing's elite get going. Numerous *kermesses* (circuit races) across the country provide a tough challenge for all levels of rider.

It's difficult to explain why cycle sport is so popular in Belgium, but the passion and engagement are truly exceptional, and leave an indelible impression on visiting cycling fans. Ghent, in particular, is a good base from which to explore Flanders during the Classics season. Indeed, the Omloop Het Nieuwsblad (formerly Omloop Het Volk, until the newspaper sponsorship changed) starts and ends in Ghent's main square. In March, there's the Gent–Wevelgem (which actually starts in nearby Deinze), while the main event, the one-day Ronde van Vlaanderen (Tour of Flanders), has employed both Antwerp and Ghent as start or finish points over the years.

The Ronde van Vlaanderen's birth in 1913 marked the start of cycling in Flanders as we know it. Before that, velodromes had been closing and the Liège–Bastogne–Liège in the Francophone south was Belgium's only top-class cycle race. But in 1912 a Flandrian, Odiel Defraeye, won the Tour de France, and the upsurge that followed led to the establishment of *Sportwereld*, a weekly sporting magazine. A promising young journalist, Karel Van Wijnendaele, set the Ronde up as a publicity stunt for the paper. These days, the Ronde is renowned for its steep, cobbled climbs (the Koppenberg, Muur-Kapelmuur, Bosberg, and others) around Oudenaarde, south of Ghent. Oudenaarde is also where you'll find the **Centrum Ronde Van Vlaanderen**, a museum dedicated to the race, where Freddy Maertens, a legendary Flandrian hardman of the 1970s, now works.

It's a pleasant 30km (17-mile) car-free cycle down the canal and the Scheldt from Ghent – join the canal path at Stropkaai, to the east of Citadelpark, and keep heading south. Stop for a drink at **De Meersbloem**, where there's a memorial to Wouter Weylandt, a local professional cyclist with Leopard-Trek who died during the Giro d'Italia in 2011. Weylandt often joined the local group rides, which meet at Adolphe della Faillelaan bridge, a few kilometres south of Ghent (if you're cycling down the river, it's identified

as Zwijnaardekasteelbrug on its span). Saturday mornings are training rides, while Wednesday evening is smash-up night. Turn up if you
dare, or for a link to more training routes and exploring ideas, head to
the Links and Addresses section (p. 58).

FAMOUS RIDERS, FAMOUS RACES

You're likely to see pro riders, feeder teams and a lot of fearsomely
good domestic club riders when out on the bike, especially around
Ghent and Oudenaarde. Tyler Farrar, the American sprinter, lived as a
neo-pro in the area and settled in Ghent afterwards, and Thomas De
Gendt also lives nearby. As for Antwerp, Rik Van Steenbergen was
born and lived in the city for many years, while Rik Van Looy and
Herman Van Springel, two Belgian heroes of the 1950s and '60s, along
with Edwig Van Hooydonck, twice winner of the Ronde, are all also
from the Antwerp area, to name just a few.

Given its proximity, the Tour de France spends a lot of time in
Belgium. The race finished in Ghent in 2007, as the *peloton* made its
way back to its normal stomping grounds after a prologue in London
and first stage to Canterbury. Antwerp featured on the route in 2010,

a boisterous *ville de passage* in the first stage from Rotterdam to Brussels. Before that, however, you have to go back to the 1950s – an overnight stop in 1954, when one stage finished in Brasschaat and the next started in Beveren (both suburbs of Antwerp); while Ghent was a *ville étape* in 1951 and *ville départ* in 1958, when the great André Darrigade won the sprint. The Giro d'Italia has not stopped at either Antwerp or Ghent, and more surprisingly, neither has featured as a stage stop in the Eneco Tour of Benelux. In 2012, however, Belgian pro cyclist Tom Boonen was first over the line in Antwerp during the initial stage of the inaugural World Ports Classic race, taking the overall win back in Rotterdam the next day.

TRACK AND 'CROSS

As any Belgian cycling aficionado will tell you, there's more to life than road cycling – principally track cycling and cyclocross. For the latter, Antwerp has the **Scheldecross,** held on the beach at Wandeldijk, within the city limits, while Ghent is close to another sand-based cyclocross race, the **Duinencross Koksijde**. Taking place at a former army base on the coast, it pits riders against the steep slopes and strength-sapping

sands of the Koksijde dunes. Duinencross is a World Cup race, which usually takes place the same weekend as the **Six Days of Ghent** track event, one of the most boisterous of the remaining Sixes. Although the Six Day event doesn't attract the huge names it used to (Bradley Wiggins won in 2001), as modern stars tend to avoid the demands of the circuit, **'t Kuipke**, the velodrome near Citadelaan, is always heaving with cycling fanatics over the six nights of action.

Get the lowdown on what's happening each evening from the locals at **Café De Karper** (p. 43), a bar owned by Ronie Keisse, father of local hero Iljo Keisse, multiple winner in 't Kuipke and road cyclist for Omega Pharma-QuickStep. Keisse, Sr. used to run the Blaarmeersen velodrome, an outdoor track built for the 1988 Track World Cup, which has since metamorphosed into the **Cycling Centre Eddy Merckx** (p. 42), one of Belgium's foremost track facilities.

Antwerp, in its day, was one of Europe's premiere track venues; its 'Garden City' velodrome in De Zurenborg was built for the 1920 Summer Olympics. The 400m (1,312 ft) track could accommodate 14,000 spectators. In the Merksem district of Antwerp is the **Sportpaleis**, a 250m (820 ft) wooden oval built in 1932. It was the largest sports hall of its time and is still in use today, albeit more for concerts than for racing. Stan Ockers, a local hero born in the suburb of Borgerhout, was World Champion when he crashed at the Sportpaleis in 1956; he died a few days later. In 1969, Jacques Anquetil also ended his professional career on the boards in Antwerp, but in less sad circumstances. After retiring, he claimed to have only ridden his bike three more times.

SPARES AND REPAIRS

De Vélodrome is a friendly bike shop in Antwerp's De Zurenborg neighbourhood. It runs a cycling team, as well as shop rides, if you're looking for company. Try also **L'Expres** or, if you're out on a ride, **Bicyclette** in nearby Duffel is a nice shop. **Plum** in the centre of Ghent is an old-school bike shop with a prestigious history of frame-building and racing (try to take a peek into the basement), while **PDG Bikestore** in nearby Drongen and **Het Verzet** in Deinze have a good range of high-end parts.

ESSENTIAL BIKE INFO

Cycling in Belgium is easy and stress-free, but there are a few things to be aware of to ensure your trip goes as smoothly as possible.

ETIQUETTE

Belgium is perhaps the ideal place to ride a bike around. Both Antwerp and Ghent have reasonably small, friendly town centres, good roads (barring the odd cobble), and a bike-mad population. The local cyclists are relaxed, but they are used to good cycling etiquette:

- Always indicate that you're about to turn. It will give people behind you the time to make allowances for your manoeuvre.
- Cycle on the right-hand side of the bike lane, so other cyclists can overtake you.
- Generally, cyclists will stop at red lights, including bicycle-specific traffic lights, which you will sometimes see in bike lanes.

SAFETY

Both Antwerp and Ghent are very safe to get around by bike, and although there are fewer dedicated bike lanes than in Amsterdam and Copenhagen, cars will unfailingly be aware of your presence. Drivers turning across a segregated bike path will not encroach on your space. There are, however, a few things to watch out for:

- Bikes are often allowed up one-way streets. If there's a 'no entry' sign, but another sign showing a bicycle and the word *Uitgezonderd*, then it's OK – bikes are excepted.
- Be careful on the cobbles. In parts of Ghent especially they can be very rough and pinch-flat thin tyres, or judder cyclists off balance.
- Pay attention to tram lines, which can trap skinny tyres and are slippery when wet. Trams have the right of way!
- You'll sometimes see scooters in bike lanes, so do not be surprised and wobble off.

- Belgian cyclists are pretty relaxed, but following the etiquette points above will help keep you out of the way of bumps with bikes and scooters.
- Use lights after dark – the police take a dim view of people who don't.

SECURITY

While Belgian cities undoubtedly suffer from bike theft, it doesn't seem as endemic as elsewhere. Hire bikes should come with a sturdy chain lock. It's advisable to lock your bike to something immovable if you're going to leave it unattended; many *Gentenaars* and *Antwerpenaars* simply chain the bike to itself, or use the wheel lock integrated into most frames, but this seems an avoidable risk. In Ghent's city centre especially, there are so many bikes around it can be difficult to find a railing or bike stand to lock to, but it's a good idea to do so – and if you've come to town with a valuable bike, it's essential. Think about using two locks, so that opportunist bike thieves will move on to an easier target.

FINDING YOUR WAY

Antwerp is well served by signposts. In the city centre, there are numerous pedestrian maps on display panels, and bike-route destinations are generally well flagged. Ghent is trickier, and can get confusing because of its winding streets and canals, but the centre is so small you won't get really lost. Keep a map handy, and you'll never be further than 15 minutes away from where you want to be. In Antwerp, if you need to get up- or downtown in a rush, take the bike path along the Scheldt. It's an expressway that will speed you north or south – just dive back into town when you're at a similar latitude to your destination.

CITY BIKES AND BIKE HIRE

Antwerp has a city bike scheme, **Velo Antwerpen**, whose distinctive red, small-wheeled bikes can be found at more than 400 stations around the city. To get a swipe card, go to the **Velo Antwerpen shop** in Antwerpen-Centraal station (p. 25), sign some forms and you'll be on your way. Or you can sign up with a credit card online and you'll get a user ID and PIN. Once you have a bike, you can use it for free for the first half hour. Any longer, and the costs will rise incrementally: 50¢ for the next half an hour, €1 for the next, and then dramatically more after that. The idea is that you use a bike for a short distance, dock it, then take another when you need it, ensuring that bikes are kept in circulation.

Alternatively, there are many places in both cities where you can rent a bike. **Antwerp Bikes** is good for a Dutch-style city bike; in Ghent, we recommend **Biker**. If you're planning to be in Belgium often, for an annual subscription **Blue Bike** gives you access to hire bikes at major stations across the country, including Antwerpen-Centraal, Antwerpen-Berchem, Gent-Sint-Pieters and Gent-Dampoort. It's simple to do, and there's more information on the website. For a road bike near Ghent, try **Het Verzet** (p. 53) in Deinze, or **PDG Bikestore** (p. 53) in Drongen. We couldn't find anywhere in Antwerp, but ask, perhaps in one of the recommended bike shops in town and see if they can help out (see the Racing and Training section for details). At **Ligfiets**, which has branches in both Antwerp and Ghent, you can, if you wish, hire a recumbent bike.

OTHER PUBLIC TRANSPORT

Buses and trams in Antwerp and Ghent do not allow bikes, but you can take an unfolded bike on local Belgian trains with a bike ticket, at any time outside the morning and evening rush hour. Just be sure to buy the bike ticket before you get on the train.

TRAVELLING TO BELGIUM WITH BIKES

By train is the safest way to travel internationally with a bike. Ghent connects to the international rail network via either Antwerp or Brussels; Antwerp is on the main line from Paris to Amsterdam and is well served by international trains. There are direct services to Paris, Rotterdam and Amsterdam. At Brussels, you can catch the **Eurostar**, or head to Germany. Cities in Austria and Switzerland connect via Cologne, Italy connects via Paris, and you can travel from further afield on sleeper trains. One non-cycling point to note: Belgium is a bilingual country, and place names are different in French and Flemish, with no quarter given to the unwary. So, if you are transferring from Brussels, the train will probably be advertised for Anvers, rather than Antwerpen (similarly Gand, rather than Gent).

When taking high-speed international Thalys, TGV and Fiera trains, bikes must be disassembled and carried in a bike bag. There are size restrictions on luggage, but most bike bags comply, and restrictions are also rarely enforced. In addition, the large luggage racks mean the whole business is fairly hassle-free. Two strategies seem to work: either race to the front of the queue, so that you can be sure of securing the space you want in the rack; or, if your bike bag is fairly slimline, wait until everyone else has stowed their luggage, and slide it in on top.

There are a couple of exceptions to this rule that may affect your journey. Firstly, as of 2013, only folding bikes in bags less than 85cm (33 in.) in length can be taken as carry-on luggage onto Eurostar trains. Instead, you must either book it a place (currently £30 per journey; it will be hung on a hook in the goods van – you can then take it on a local Belgian train if you buy a bike ticket), or put it in a bag and send it via the registered baggage service. The 'Turn Up and Go' option, where you leave your bike bag at a counter in the check-in hall, costs £10 each way. Secondly, German Intercity-Express (ICE) trains will not allow bike bags bigger than 85cm (33 in.) in any dimension, which essentially rules out any non-folding bikes. German Intercity (IC) and Eurocity (EC) trains allow bikes to be wheeled on board if you pay for a reservation, so it's best to factor in a non-high-speed train if you're intending to travel to Belgium from Germany. All trains allow folding bikes, though on ICE trains these must again be bagged.

The small, international **Antwerp Airport** is only 7km (4 miles) from the centre of town, so you could, in theory, cycle to and from your flight along bike paths. The airport is southeast of the centre: at **Antwerpen-Berchem station**, head over Borsbeekbrug (straight on from Cogels-Osylei), and over the ring road. Follow Diksmuidelaan and immediately take the left fork along Gitschotellei, which will take you eventually to the airport.

LINKS AND ADDRESSES

Ann Demeulemeester
Leopold de Waelplaats,
2000 Antwerp
anndemeulemeester.be

Antiek Depot
Baudelostraat 15, 9000, Ghent
antiek-depot.com

Antwerps Justitiepaleis
Bolivarplaats 20, 2000 Antwerp

Aqua Azul
Drongenhof 2, 9000 Ghent
aqua-azul.be

Atelier Solarshop
Dambruggestraat 48,
2060 Antwerp
ateliersolarshop.blogspot.com

Badboot
Van de Mexicobruggen,
2000 Antwerp
badboot.be

Bakkerij Goossens
Korte Gasthuisstraat 31,
2000 Antwerp

Barista
Hippoliet Lippensplein 25,
9000 Ghent

Battle of Waterloo mosaic
Waterloostraat 11, 2600 Antwerp

Blaarmeersen
Watersportslaan, 9000 Ghent
gent.be/blaarmeersen

Bocadero
Rijnkaai 150, 2000 Antwerp
bocadero.be

Bord'eau
Sint-Veerleplein 5, 9000 Ghent
oudevismijn.be

Bourgoyen-Ossemeersen
Driepikkelstraat 32, 9030 Ghent

Brooderie
Jan Breydelstraat 8, 9000 Ghent
brooderie.be

Café Beveren
Vlasmarkt 2, 2000 Antwerp

Café d'Anvers
Verversrui 15, 2000 Antwerp
cafe-d-anvers.com

Café De Karper
Kortrijksesteenweg 2,
9000 Ghent
cafedekarper.be

Café De Loge
Annonciadenstraat 5,
9000 Ghent
deloge.be

Café Hopper
Leopold de Waelstraat 2,
2000 Antwerp
cafehopper.be

Café Noord
Grote Markt 24, 2000 Antwerp

Café Vertigo
Draakplaats 3, 2018 Antwerp
cafevertigo.be

Café Video
Oude Beestenmarkt 7,
9000 Ghent
cafevideo.be

Caffènation
Hopland 46, 2000 Antwerp
caffenation.be

Caravan Eetcafé
Damplein 17, 2060 Antwerp
decaravan.be

Cargo
Viaduct-Dam 64–80,
2060 Antwerp
cargozomerbar.be

Céleste
Hoogstraat 77, 2000 Antwerp
celeste-antwerp.be

Charlatan
Vlasmarkt 6, 9000 Ghent
charlatan.be

Chatleroi
Graaf van Hoornestraat 2,
2000 Antwerp
chatleroi.be

Clinic
De Burburestraat 5,
2000 Antwerp
clinicantwerp.com

Coffee & Vinyl
Volkstraat 45, 2000 Antwerp
vinylrecords.be

Damme Patisserie
Nederkouter 139, 9000 Ghent
createursdedesserts.be

De Biologisch-Dynamische Bakkerij
Volkstraat 17, 2000 Antwerp

De Burgerij
Tramplein 2, 2600 Berchem
burgerij.be

De Meersbloem
Zwartekobenstraat 32,
9052 Zwijnaarde

Den Turk
Botermarkt 3, 9000 Ghent
cafedenturk.be

Dépôt Central
Lammerstraat 15, 9000 Ghent
polepole.be/cafe/depot

Designcenter de Winkelhaak
Lange Winkelhaakstraat 26,
2060 Antwerp
winkelhaak.be

Design Museum Gent
Jan Breydelstraat 5, 9000 Ghent
designmuseumgent.be

Désiré de Lille
Schrijnwerkersstraat 14,
2000 Antwerp
desiredelille.be

Dock's Café
Jordaenskaai 7, 2000 Antwerp
docks.be

DOK
Splitsing Koopvaardijlaan,
Afrikalaan, 9000 Ghent
dokgent

Dôme
Grote Hondstraat 2,
2018 Antwerp
domeweb.be

Domestic
Steenbokstraat 37, 2018 Antwerp
domeweb.be

Dôme sur Mer
Arendstraat 1, 2018 Antwerp
domeweb.be

Dries Van Noten
Nationalestraat 16,
2000 Antwerp
driesvannoten.be

Eetcafé Cabo Verde
Napelstraat 116, 2000 Antwerp
eetcafecaboverde.be

Espressobar Broer Bretel
Nassaustraat 7, 2000 Antwerp
broerbretel.be

FCS
Timmerwerfstraat 8,
2000 Antwerp

Fiskebar
Marnixplaats 12, 2000 Antwerp
fiskebar.be

FotoMuseum
Waalsekaai 47, 2000 Antwerp
fotomuseum.be

Four Seasons houses
Generaal van Merlenstraat
27–30, 2600 Antwerp

FoxHole
Reyndersstraat 10, 2000 Antwerp
foxholeshop.com

Frituur Jozef
Vrijdagmarkt, 9000 Ghent

Frituur No. 1
Hoogstraat 1, 2000 Antwerp

Grand Café Horta
Hopland 2, 2000 Antwerp
grandcafehorta.be

Gravensteen Castle
Sint-Veerleplein 11, 9000 Ghent
gent.be

Gruut Stadsbrouwerij
Grote Huidevettershoek 10,
9000 Ghent
gruut.be

Haute Frituur
Vlaamse Kaai 66, 2000 Antwerp

Het Archief
Steendam 110, 9000 Ghent
het-archief.be

Het Hinkelspel
Ferdinand Lousbergskaai 33,
9000 Ghent
hethinkelspel.be

Het Pomphuis
Siberiastraat z/n, 2030 Antwerp
hetpomphuis.be

Het Velootje Gent
Kalversteeg 2, 9000 Ghent
tvelootje.mine.nu

Hoffy's
Lange Kievitstraat 52,
2018 Antwerp
hoffys.be

Holy Corner
Begijnhofdries, 9000 Ghent
elisabethbegijnhof.be

Hospital
De Burburestraat 4,
2000 Antwerp
hospital-antwerp.com

Huize Colette
Belfortstraat 6, 9000 Ghent

**International Gemological
Institute**
Schupstraat 1, 2018 Antwerp
igiworldwide.com

KBC Tower
Eiermarkt 20, 2000 Antwerp

King Kong
Volkstraat 58, 2000 Antwerp

KMSKA
Leopold de Waelplaats,
2000 Antwerp
kmska.be

Komkommertijd
Reep 14, 9000 Ghent
komkommertijd.be

Kulminator
Vleminckveld 32, 2000 Antwerp

Labels, Inc.
Aalmoezenierstraat 4,
2000 Antwerp
labelsinc.be

Le Jardin Bohémien
Burgstraat 19, 9000 Ghent
lejardinbohemien.be

Lekker GEC
Koningin Maria
Hendrikaplein 4-5, 9000 Ghent
lekkergec.be

L'Entrepôt du Congo
Vlaamse Kaai 42, 2000 Antwerp
entrepotducongo.com

Ligfiets
Steenhouwersvest 25,
2000 Antwerp
ligfiets.be

Lombardia
Lombardenvest 78, 2000
Antwerp
lombardia.be

Marimain
Walpoortstraat 17, 9000 Ghent

McQueen
Korte Koepoortstraat 2,
2000 Antwerp
mcqueen.be

Middelheimmuseum
Middelheimlaan 61,
2020 Antwerp
middelheimmuseum.be

ModeMuseum
Nationalestraat 28,
2000 Antwerp
momu.be

ModeNatie
Nationalestraat 28,
2000 Antwerp
modenatie.com

Mokabon
Donkersteeg 35, 9000 Ghent
mokabon.be

Moskou
Draakplaats 5, 2018 Antwerp
brasseriemoskou.be

Mosquito Coast
Hoogpoort 28, 9000 Ghent
mosquitocoast.be

MuKHA
Leuvenstraat 32, 2000 Antwerp
muhka.be

Museum Aan de Stroom
Hanzestedenplaats 1,
2000 Antwerp
mas.be

Museum Mayer van den Bergh
Lange Gasthuisstraat 19,
2000 Antwerp
mayervandenbergh.be

Noë
Kloosterstraat 90, 2000 Antwerp
your-antwerp.com/tag/noe

NormoCoffee
Minderbroedersrui 30,
2000 Antwerp
normocoffee.be

Nottebohm
Biartstraat 2, 2018 Antwerp
nottebohm.be

OR Espressobar
Walpoortstraat 26, 9000 Ghent
orcoffee.be

Oud Huis Himschoot
Groentenmarkt 1, 9000 Ghent
bakkerijhimschoot.be

Pain Perdu
Walpoortstraat 9, 9000 Ghent

Park Spoor Noord
parkspoornoord.com

Plantin-Moretus Museum
Vrijdagmarkt 22, 2000 Antwerp
museumplantinmoretus.be

Quetzal
Sint-Pietersnieuwstraat 99,
9000 Ghent
quetzal.be

RA
Kloosterstraat 13, 2000 Antwerp
ra13.be

Radio Minerva
Wandeldijk 20, 2050 Antwerp
radio-minerva.be

Red Star Line Museum
Falconrui 53, 2000 Antwerp
redstarline.be

Réfectoire
Plantin en Moretuslei 73,
2018 Antwerp
refectoire.be

Revista
Karel Rogierstraat 47,
2000 Antwerp

Rubenshuis
Wapperplein 9/–11,
2000 Antwerp
rubenshuis.be

Second Life
Keistraat 1, 2000 Antwerp
**retrowinkelsecondlife.webs.
com**

Sint-Baafskathedraal
Sint-Baafsplein, 9000 Ghent
sintbaafskathedraal.be

Sint-Felix warehouse
Oudeleeuwenrui 29,
2000 Antwerp
felixarchief.be

Sint-Jacobskerk (Antwerp)
Lange Nieuwstraat 73,
2000 Antwerp

Sint-Jacobskerk (Ghent)
9000 Ghent
mkaweb.be

Sint-Pietersabdij
Sint-Pietersplein 9, 9000 Ghent
sintpietersabdijgent.be

Sips
Gillisplaats 8, 2000 Antwerp
sips-cocktails.com

SMAK
Nicolaas de Liemaeckereplein 2,
9000 Ghent
smak.be

Stadhuis
Grote Markt 1, 2000 Antwerp
antwerpen.be

Starfish & Coffee
Bresstraat 9, 2018 Antwerp
**starfishandcoffeeantwerpen.
blogspot.com**

Steinerschool
Volkstraat 40, 2000 Antwerp
steinerschoolantwerpen.be

Suite
Hoogpoort 59, 9000 Ghent
suite-gent.be

Surplus
Zwartezustersstraat 9,
9000 Ghent
surplusinterieur.be

't Brantyser
Hendrik Conscienceplein 7,
2000 Antwerp
brantyser.be

't Elfde Gebod
Torfbrug 10, 2000 Antwerp
kathedraalcafe.be

't Fritkotje
Londenstraat 48, 2000 Antwerp
fritkotje.be

The Fallen Angels
Jan Breydelstraat 29,
9000 Ghent
the-fallen-angels.com

Toykyo
Hoogpoort 11, 9000 Ghent
toykyo.be

't Waagstuk
Stadswaag 20, 2000 Antwerp
waagstuk.be

Vinicity
Karel Rogierstraat 40,
2000 Antwerp
vinicity.com

Vooruit
Sint-Pietersnieuwstraat 23,
9000 Ghent
vooruit.be

Waanzee
Sint-Aldegondiskaai 52,
2018 Antwerp

Walrus
Jan van Beersstraat 2,
2018 Antwerp
eetcafewalrus.com

Walter
Sint-Antoniusstraat 12,
2000 Antwerp
waltervanbeirendonck.com

Ydee
Oudburg 56, 9000 Ghent
ydee.be

Yellow Submarine
Falconplein 51, 2000 Antwerp
yellowsubmarine.be

Your
Kloosterstraat 90,
2000 Antwerp
your-antwerp.com

Zeezicht
Dageraadplaats 7, 2018 Antwerp
cafezeezicht.be

Zuiderterras
Ernest Van Dijckkaai 37,
2000 Antwerp
zuiderterras.be

BIKES SHOPS, CLUBS, RACES AND VENUES

For links to our racing and training routes, please visit citycyclingguides.com

Antwerp Bikes
antwerpbikes.be

Bicyclette
Merodestraat 1, 2570 Duffel
bicyclette.cc

Bike Project
Lange Koepoortstraat 5, 2000
bikeproject.be

Biker
Steendam 16, 9000
bikerfietsen.be

Blue Bike
blue-bike.be

Centrum Ronde van Vlaanderen
Markt 43, 9700 Oudenaarde
crvv.be

Cycling Centre Eddy Merckx
Zuiderlaan 8, 9000
eddymerckx.be

De Vélodrome
Dageraadplaats 34, 2018 Antwerp
develodrome.be

Duinencross Koksijde
8670 Koksijde
uci.ch

Fixerati
Lange Koepoortstraat 13, 2000
fixerati.com

Het Verzet
Nieuwstraat 41, 9800 Deinze
hetverzet.be

L'Expres
Hessenbrug 2, 2000 Antwerp
lexpres.com

PDG Bikestore
Baarledorpstraat 29, 9031 Drongen
pdgbikestore.be

Plum
Nederkouter 141, 9000 Ghent
plum-gent.com

Scheldecross Antwerpen
sport.be.msn.com/cyclocrossclassics

Six Days of Ghent
Het Kuipke, Citadelpark, 9000 Ghent
z6sdaagse.be

Sportpaleis
Schijnpoortweg 119, 2170 Merksem
sportpaleis.be

't Kuipke
Citadelpark, 9000 Ghent

Velo Antwerpen
Antwerpen-Centraal station, Diamond Gallery, Entrance Kievitplein, 2018 Antwerp
velo-antwerpen.be

OTHER USEFUL SITES

Antwerp Airport
Luchthavenlei z/n, 2100
antwerp-airport.be

Antwerpen-Berchem station
Burgemeester Edgar Ryckaertsplein 1, 2600, Berchem
hari.b-holding.be

Antwerpen-Centraal station
Koningin Astridplein 27, 2018
hari.b-holding.be

Eurostar
eurostar.com

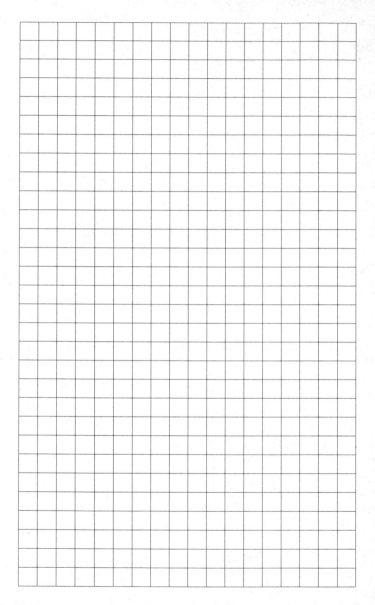

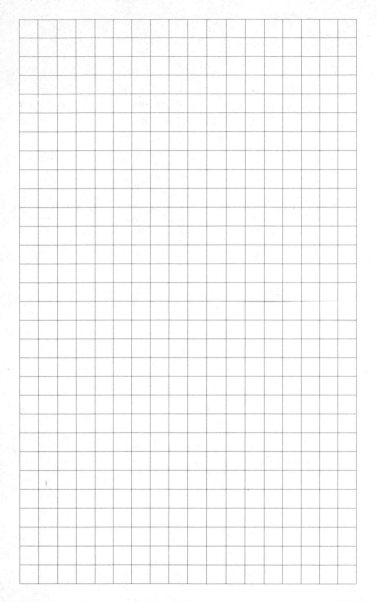

63

Rapha, established in London, has always been a champion of city cycling – from testing our first prototype jackets on the backs of bike couriers, to a whole range of products designed specifically for the demands of daily life on the bike. As well as an online emporium of products, films, photography and stories, Rapha has a growing network of Cycle Clubs, locations around the globe where cyclists can enjoy live racing, food, drink and products. Rapha is also the official clothing supplier of Team Sky, the world's leading cycling team.

Rapha.